SAUNDERS
BOOK COMPANY

Published by Saunders Book Company
27 Stewart Road
Collingwood ON Canada L9Y 4M7

DESIGN AND PRODUCTION BY **ZENO DESIGN**

Printed in the United States of America

PHOTOGRAPHS BY Alamy (John Angerson, David Crausby,
Danita Delimont, dk, foodfolio, Kevin Foy, Joeysworld.com,
Chuck Pefley, Peter Adams Photography, WorldFoto), Corbis
(Peter Adams, Daren Fentiman/ZUMA, Reuters), Getty
Images (Tim Boyle, ColorBlind Images, Mitchell Funk, Dave
Hogan, Suzane Opton//Time Life Pictures, Spencer Platt,
Justin Sullivan, Wallace and Wyant)

LIBRARY OF CONGRESS CATALOGING-IN-PUBLICATION DATA

Gilbert, Sara.
The story of Starbucks / by Sara Gilbert.
p. cm. — (Built for success)
Includes index
ISBN-13: 978-1-897563-07-6 (pbk.)
1. Starbucks Coffee Company—Juvenile literature. 2. Coffee
industry—United States—Juvenile literature. I. Title.

HD9199.U52S734 2008
338.7'616479573—dc22   2007014995

First edition

9 8 7 6 5 4 3 2 1

BUILT FOR SUCCESS

THE STORY OF

Starbucks

SARA GILBERT

On August 18, 1987, Howard Schultz walked into the Seattle, Washington, roasting plant of the Starbucks Coffee Company. Fresh beans were rattling through the roasters, filling the space with a warm, comforting aroma. Schultz, who had just purchased the assets of the company for $4 million, stood before his new employees and told them about his plan to turn the regional coffee roaster with only a handful of retail outlets into a national chain of coffee shops. He was convinced that he could turn the company's success in Seattle into a national phenomenon, that the appeal of a steaming cup of coffee was almost universal. "I'm here today because I love this company," he said as he laid out the business plan. "I love what it represents."

CHAPTER ONE

Bags of Beans, Cups of Coffee

Howard Schultz was turned down the first time he interviewed for a job at Starbucks. It was the spring of 1982, and the young salesman from New York had made a trip out to Seattle to try to convince Jerry Baldwin and Gordon Bowker, the founders of Starbucks Coffee Company, to hire hire him as **marketing** manager.

But the company, which had been selling fresh roasted coffee beans by the pound since 1971, primarily in the Pacific Northwest but also by mail order, turned down Schultz's ambitious plan to make their company known from coast to coast. "It's risky, too much change," Baldwin, the president of the company, told him.

Schultz was devastated. He had fallen in love with both the company's product and its laid-back, friendly culture during a tour of the plant, and he was convinced that with a little help, it could become a nationally known **brand**. He was prepared to take a pay cut and move to Seattle to work for the company. In fact, he was determined to do so. So the next day, Schultz called back and made another pitch for his services. "The destiny of Starbucks is at stake," Schultz said. This time it worked. He was hired as the director of retail operations and marketing for Starbucks.

In his first year, Schultz did everything from helping out behind the counter at the company's retail outlets to working on customer-service skills with the sales staff.

New Yorker Howard Schultz found success in Seattle, becoming a billionaire through Starbucks

But in his second year with the company, he traveled to Milan, Italy, for an international housewares trade show, a trip that changed his whole opinion about coffee consumption. While in Milan, Schultz visited several **espresso** bars where hot, strong coffee drinks—espressos, caffe lattes, and cappuccinos—were being served by graceful **baristas**. The coffee was incredible, but the atmosphere was even better: Although most of the bars were crowded, the customers laughed and joked with the staff as if they were friends. There was an energy, a sense of camaraderie, and a feeling of romance that Schultz immediately appreciated.

When Schultz returned to Seattle, he suggested that Starbucks duplicate the espresso-bar concept. But Baldwin and Bowker didn't want to dilute their core business, which was roasting and selling the best coffee beans possible. Again, however, Schultz wouldn't take no for an answer. Finally, in April 1984, Baldwin allowed him to test the concept in a tiny, 300-square-foot (27.8 sq m) section of a Starbucks retail outlet in downtown Seattle. About 400 people passed through the store the first day it served coffee by the cup; within two months, that number had doubled. Baristas couldn't keep up with the lines of customers who wanted a steaming cup of coffee.

Each day, Schultz took a detailed sales report and customer count to Baldwin. "The customers are telling us something," Schultz told him. "This is a big idea. We've got to keep moving on it." Still, Baldwin was adamant that coffee bars were not going to be part of the Starbucks business plan. "We're coffee roasters. I don't want to be in the restaurant business," he told Schultz. Although he offered to put a few espresso machines in the back of some stores, his final decision was that Starbucks was not going to become a chain of espresso bars.

When Schultz realized that he wasn't going to win, he made a decision of his own: He would have to leave Starbucks and start another company that would serve coffee and espresso drinks. His stores, he hoped, would recreate the romance he had experienced in Italy—and so he gave them an Italian

Howard Schultz discovered his coffee-making inspiration in the bustling coffee shops and bars of Europe

name: Il Giornale (pronounced *eel jor-NAH-lee*), which means "newspaper," or "daily." Early in 1985, he told Starbucks owners, including Jerry Baldwin, about his plan and announced that he would leave the company at the end of the year. Baldwin and Bowker supported Schultz's decision to break off on his own. They even decided to invest $150,000 of Starbucks' cash in Il Giornale, telling Schultz that they thought his business plan was strong.

Baldwin and Bowker's support meant almost as much as their money to Schultz, who still had to raise about $1.7 million more to get his idea—a chain of Italian-style coffeehouses spread across the country—off the ground. By January 1986, he had raised $400,000 in **seed money**, enough to open a first store in Seattle. Schultz's hope was that once that store was up and running, it would be easier to attract **investors**. They would be able to see the beauty of the design and taste the quality of the coffee, and Schultz was confident that would be enough to earn the rest of the money needed to expand the business.

On April 8, 1986, the first Il Giornale store opened in downtown Seattle. On its first day of business, almost 300 customers stopped by. Within six months, the store was serving about 1,000 people a day—many of them regulars who had even learned how to pronounce Il Giornale correctly. A second Seattle store opened in October; in April 1987, a third store, in Vancouver, British Columbia, was up and running. By the middle of 1987, sales at Il Giornale were close to $500,000 a year. Although he was not yet making a profit, Schultz could almost taste the success in his morning cup of coffee.

> *"We're in the business of human connection and humanity, creating communities in a third place between home and work."*
>
> STARBUCKS FOUNDER HOWARD SCHULTZ

Howard Schultz hoped customers would come for their Il Giornale coffee like they did their daily newspaper.

Original Starbucks logo in Pikes Place market

THE MEANING OF THE MERMAID

The striking green, black, and white logo that adorns all Starbucks products is a salute to the company's earliest incarnation. When Starbucks Coffee Company was formed in 1971 as a coffee bean roaster and retailer, it took its name from Herman Melville's seafaring novel *Moby Dick* —the first mate on the infamous ship the *Pequod* (which was also suggested as a name for the company but was roundly rejected) was named Starbuck. The plan was to pair the logo with the name, so the original owners based its design on a 16th-century Nordic woodcut of a two-tailed mermaid. When Howard Schultz bought the company and its name in 1987, he changed the mermaid from brown to green and later reduced the framing to her head and upper body (the original had exposed breasts and belly button). The original logo can still be seen on the Starbucks store in Seattle's Pikes Place market.

CHAPTER TWO

Starting over as Starbucks

Just as Schultz was beginning to see the fruits of his labors at Il Giornale, he was surprised to find out that Starbucks was for sale. Baldwin and Bowker had both developed other business interests and wanted to leave the company. Schultz knew that he had to buy Starbucks from his friends and former employers.

To do so, however, he had to come up with almost $4 million not even a year after rounding up $1.25 million to start Il Giornale. But when Schultz went back to his investors, he found that they were again willing to help him raise funds for the purchase. Within a matter of weeks, he had the $3.8 million asking price. On August 15, 1987, Schultz officially took ownership of Starbucks.

Schultz had bought more than a building full of coffee beans, though. Part of the purchase included the Starbucks name. And because Starbucks had a much longer history than his Il Giornale operation, and twice as many retail outlets (six stores, compared to three Il Giornales), Schultz quickly decided to rename his business Starbucks Corporation.

The decision to take Starbucks outside of Seattle was settled almost as quickly. Schultz had ambitiously promised investors that Starbucks would open 125 new stores within 5 years. He had also announced his plans to expand into the national market when he addressed the company's employees on his first day as owner,

Coffee plants are grown in tropical locales such as Hawaii and South America, and the beans exported

saying they would all be witnesses to the beginning of something great. "In five years, I want you to look back on this day and say, 'I was there when it started. I helped build this company into something great,'" he told them. And before 1987 was over, he would take Starbucks to untested territory: Chicago, Illinois.

It was a risky move. Starbucks had name recognition in the Pacific Northwest, but very few people in America's heartland had ever heard of the company. Chicago was 2,000 miles (3,218 km) away from the roasting plant, creating a logistical nightmare for a company that demanded only the freshest beans be used in its coffee. Friends also warned Schultz that midwesterners were more likely to stop at a gas station for a cup of inexpensive coffee than to pay $2 or more for a latte or cappuccino.

Schultz, however, figured that Chicago's cold winter climate made it an ideal place to sell hot drinks. And it was large enough to allow for several stores within the same city. So, in October 1987, he opened a Starbucks a block away from the Sears Tower in downtown Chicago; within six months, three more Starbucks popped up in the city. Unfortunately, none of them fared particularly well. The first would close a few years after it opened.

Even as the Chicago stores were losing money, however, Starbucks continued its aggressive expansion plan. By the end of 1987, there were 17 stores in Seattle, Chicago, and Vancouver, British Columbia; 16 more opened in those same markets in 1988. In 1989, as 20 new stores opened in the Pacific Northwest and in Chicago, the company figured out how to solve a nagging problem that could have hindered its expansion: how to keep coffee beans that had been roasted at the Seattle site fresh as they were sent across the country. The solution was FlavorLock bags, a kind of vacuum packaging with a one-way valve that allows carbon dioxide gases to pass out without letting air or moisture in. When one of the five-pound (2.27 kg) bags that were shipped out of the plant was opened several days later, the beans were just as fresh as they had been when they were put in.

Despite Chicago's big population and bustling downtown, the city was not an immediately successful coffee venue

Soon, those FlavorLock bags were being sent to Los Angeles. Despite concerns that hot drinks would never sell in Southern California's hot climate, Starbucks was an immediate hit in and around Hollywood. "Almost overnight, Starbucks became chic," Schultz later said. "Word of mouth, we discovered, is far more powerful than advertising."

By the end of 1991, 116 Starbucks stores were open across America and Canada, putting Schultz and his executive team ahead of their targeted growth. After three years of losing money, the company was even turning a tidy profit. It was time, they decided, to make Starbucks a public company with an **initial public offering** (IPO) of stock.

Schultz would later state that June 26, 1992, the day that Starbucks stock was first traded on **NASDAQ**, was the happiest day of his business career. He and several other Starbucks senior managers huddled together in the office of a stock broker in downtown Seattle, waiting for the company's **ticker symbol**— SBUX—to come up on the screen. When the stock markets opened in New York and the stock jumped from its initial price of $17 to $21, everyone in the room cheered.

Starbucks' IPO was one of the most successful of the year, raising $29 million in investments for the company and increasing its value to $273 million. But to many on New York's Wall Street, where most trading takes place, it had come out of nowhere; at the time, Starbucks hadn't gotten any farther east than Chicago. Many of the people buying and selling the company's stock that day had never even had a cup of its coffee.

> "What set Starbucks apart in the early days and today is a single-minded focus on the coffee as an end in itself. That is so different from what you usually see in the coffee trade."
>
> KEVIN KNOX, FORMER STARBUCKS COFFEE TESTER

Improved packaging that sealed in freshness was a key development in Starbucks' rapid expansion

THE FRAPPUCCINO PHENOMENON

It started in Southern California. Dina Campion, a Starbucks district manager, noticed that customers kept asking for blended icy drinks, then leaving empty-handed when they were told Starbucks didn't sell anything like that. So Campion bought a blender and started experimenting with different cold concoctions. Early in 1994, she and Dan Moore, a Starbucks partner in retail operations, presented their **prototype** to Howard Schultz. "I thought it was awful," Schultz said later. "It had a chalky, pasty taste." Soon, the recipe was being studied by a team of food consultants, who came up with a new process that started with freshly brewed coffee and lowfat milk. That version was enormously popular in taste tests—even with Schultz. The company named the drink the "Frappuccino"—a combination of "frappe," which is a frozen drink, and "cappuccino"—and introduced it nationwide in April 1995. "It was an instant hit," Schultz said, "a runaway home run."

CHAPTER THREE

Coffee on Every Corner

The influx of cash from investors meant that Starbucks could now surge ahead with its goal to become the most recognized coffee brand in the country. It opened stores in San Diego, San Francisco, and Denver, finding a receptive customer base in each city. By April 1993, with more than 165 stores already in operation, Schultz was ready to see his company cross the continent and set up shop on the East Coast.

The company chose Washington, D.C., as its first eastern city partly because it had always been a strong base for mail orders of fresh beans. There was also hope that the global nature of Washington's population, with many Europeans and others living and working there, would serve Starbucks well. That speculation was right; the first store in the city drew sizable crowds when it opened in 1993, and the second did even better. In the years that followed, that second store, in the city's busy Dupont Circle neighborhood, would become one of Starbucks' highest-volume outlets in the country.

By the end of 1994, Starbucks coffeehouses were also open in New York, Boston, Minneapolis, Atlanta, Dallas, and Houston. The company built a new roasting plant in Kent, Washington, to keep up with the demand for fresh roasted beans from its

Starbucks initially focused its expansion in the West, opening stores like this one in San Francisco

400-plus stores. Sales and earnings were soaring, and Wall Street investors were responding by increasing the value of the company's stock. In July 1993, the same month that Schultz turned 40, he appeared on the cover of *Fortune* magazine with the headline, "Howard Schultz's Starbucks grinds coffee into gold."

As Starbucks grew, so did America's appetite for specialty coffee drinks such as cappuccinos and caffe lattes. Suddenly, competing coffeehouses were sprouting up across the country. Starbucks, which was far bigger than most of the new **mom-and-pop** operations, didn't consider them to be much of a threat. Still, the company accelerated its expansion plans, especially on the East Coast, to keep its edge over the competition. By 1995, Starbucks was opening an average of one new store a day.

Just as everything was going so well, including the launch of its signature cold coffee drink, the Frappucino, and the introduction of CD sales into its stores, Starbucks faced its first major crisis. In the summer of 1994, a severe frost had hit Brazil, one of the largest coffee producers in the world. Almost a third of that country's coffee crop was damaged. Although Starbucks didn't purchase any of its beans from Brazil, importing its supply from Africa, Indonesia, and Columbia instead, it immediately felt the impact as the cost of coffee skyrocketed. Within weeks, green coffee prices jumped from about $1 a pound (.45 kg) to $2.74 a pound.

The good news was that Starbucks had locked in almost a year's supply of green coffee at the previous low prices. The bad news was that the cost increases were impacting the company's stock prices and would almost certainly affect sales figures as well, as the company had to order more beans for the coming year. The question Schultz and his executives faced was whether to raise retail prices to help offset the costs. Although the canned coffee available in grocery stores had already jumped in price, Starbucks was deeply concerned about how an increase in the prices of their drinks and beans, which were already higher than those in supermarkets, would sit with customers.

The frost that hit coffee fields in South America was eventually felt by American consumers buying bagged beans

COFFEE ON EVERY CORNER

In July 1994, the company decided to bump its prices by about 10 percent—a nickel or dime increase on most of its drinks, but more than $1 for a pound (.45 kg) of beans. It was a difficult decision, Schultz said, but the company had to somehow cover its increased costs for the coming year. And in the end, most customers didn't change their buying habits over the prices. "For the most part, they responded by being willing to pay higher prices for coffee they knew was best of class," Schultz said.

By the end of 1994, coffee prices were back down to almost $1 a pound (.45 kg). And although Starbucks' **bottom line** had suffered, the company chose not to back away from its continuing expansion plan. Instead, at the urging of company president Orin Smith, it decided to find ways to make its internal operations more efficient. The changes, including cuts in the costs of manufacturing and transporting products such as beans, cups, and other supplies, were hardly noticeable outside of the corporate headquarters in Seattle. The rest of the world saw Starbucks open up in Philadelphia and Pittsburgh, and pop up on The Strip in Las Vegas. Stores were launched in Cincinnati, Baltimore, San Antonio, and Austin, Texas—each one drawing near-capacity crowds immediately. By the end of 1995, there were 677 Starbucks locations across the U.S. and Canada.

But that was no longer good enough. Having all but conquered America, Starbucks was ready to become a worldwide purveyor of coffee drinks. In 1995, Schultz decided that it was time to go global. He appointed Howard Behar, a longtime executive, to study international expansion.

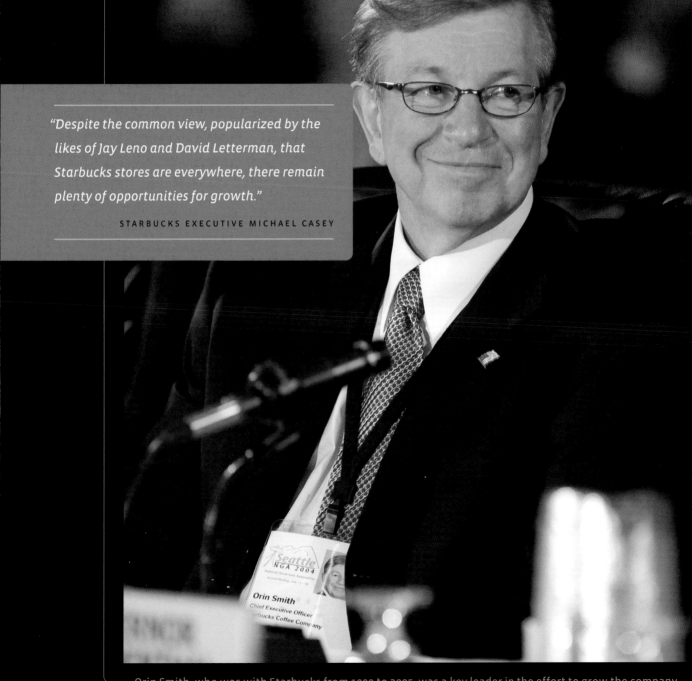

"Despite the common view, popularized by the likes of Jay Leno and David Letterman, that Starbucks stores are everywhere, there remain plenty of opportunities for growth."

STARBUCKS EXECUTIVE MICHAEL CASEY

Orin Smith, who was with Starbucks from 1990 to 2005, was a key leader in the effort to grow the company

CELEBRITY SIGHTINGS

Movie star Will Ferrell has been seen sipping out of a Starbucks cup. Singer Madonna brought a cup of Starbucks coffee with her to a reading of her children's book. Singer Jessica Simpson, talk show hosts Jay Leno and Jon Stewart, actor Renée Zellweger, and California governor Arnold Schwarzenegger have also given the brand their unofficial endorsement by carrying cups around. Such exposure, known as product placement when it's intentional, is worth millions of dollars. But Starbucks says that it doesn't pay celebrities to promote its brand, and certain stars (including actors Ben Affleck and Jennifer Garner) confirm that report. "I would be very skeptical that Starbucks paid anyone anything. It's really inconsistent with the Starbucks brand, and A-list stars like Affleck and Garner are more into building their own brands," says Gary Mezzatesta, president and CEO of UPP Entertainment Marketing. "They probably just really like the coffee. Who doesn't?"

CHAPTER FOUR

Going Global

O n August 2, 1996, Howard Schultz stood with Howard Behar, the president of Starbucks Coffee International, on a corner in Tokyo, Japan, watching a line almost 50 people deep form at the counter of the brand-new Starbucks store there.

Critics had warned the company that although the Japanese people had developed an infatuation with blue jeans, Coca-Cola, and many other American things, they would likely never warm to the concept of take-out coffee and food. But on that hot summer day in Tokyo—temperatures soared near 95 °F (35 °C), with intense humidity—many customers ordered hot lattes or espressos and walked out carrying cups with the green Starbucks logo.

By the end of 1996, three more stores were open and operating in Japan. Starbucks Coffee International, in a **joint venture** with the Japanese company SAZABY, Inc., took off from there, spreading throughout the Pacific Rim. Within five years, almost 300 stores would open; that number would double two years later. The company went public on NASDAQ's Japanese Market in 2001, capping a most successful international experiment.

Starbucks was being just as aggressive back in the U.S. in the late 1990s. It continued to spread its reach across the country, opening more stores in more states,

Starbucks reached Asia in the late 1990s, establishing stores first in Japan, then in China (pictured).

including Hawaii. At the same time, it was embarking on a series of new partnerships with other companies to further solidify its prominence. It had already worked with Capitol Records to create a series of popular music CDs that were sold exclusively in Starbucks stores and had formed a partnership with Barnes & Noble to incorporate Starbucks outlets inside their bookstores. Now it was also working with PepsiCo to bottle and market the hugely successful Frappuccino drink and partnering with Dreyer's Grand Ice Cream to develop the Starbucks Superpremium Ice Cream line. Both were so instantly popular among shoppers that it was difficult to keep the products on the shelves and in the freezers at grocery stores and supermarkets. "Sales exploded almost immediately," said Shari Fujii, the marketing manager of Starbucks' ice cream partnership. "Within four months we were selling the number one coffee ice cream flavor in the nation."

Not every partnership met with such immediate success, however. When Starbucks coffee became the official in-flight coffee for United Airlines in 1995, the company stood to more than double the number of people drinking its coffee almost overnight—an attractive opportunity. Schultz was initially reluctant to enter into the deal, voicing concern over quality control in the air, especially without trained baristas brewing the beverage. But United persisted, and he agreed to give the arrangement a try.

The initial rollout was disastrous, for all the reasons that had worried Schultz. Although Starbucks had tried to ensure that its high standards for quality brewing would be followed on the planes, the logistics were overwhelming for the airline and its crew. Their equipment had to be modified, and the coffee had to be made in outdated machines. The quality of the final product was nowhere near what customers were used to receiving in Starbucks stores—and many of them called to voice their complaints.

Within a matter of months, Starbucks and United had solved the problem with new equipment and better training for the crews. By the end of the year,

In 1995, Starbucks teamed up with Dreyer's—a 67-year-old ice cream company—to create a coffee ice cream

almost three-quarters of the passengers on United's 3,000-plus daily flights were rating the coffee served onboard as either excellent or good—and most said that it was far better than typical airline coffee.

Even with an estimated 20 million people drinking Starbucks coffee at 35,000 feet (10,670 m) above the earth each year, the company was still looking for growth. At the end of 1996, Starbucks had more than 1,000 stores worldwide. Not even five years later, at the end of the millennium, that figure was pushing 3,500, including new stores in Saudi Arabia, Australia, and Hong Kong. Profits were soaring, spurred in part by the sale of Starbucks coffee in about 18,000 grocery stores and supermarkets beginning in 1998. The company had begun **acquiring** other small businesses, including Tazo, a Portland, Oregon-based tea company, and had established the Starbucks Foundation, a charitable branch that dedicated dollars to literacy efforts and other causes.

By the middle of 2000, Starbucks had locations in all 50 states; in some cities, stores were actually located just across the street from one another. The company's big push, then, was to achieve the same sort of dominance around the world. Although the company had stores in Japan and around Asia, it hadn't yet established itself in Europe—and Schultz saw that as the next frontier. "Starbucks is going to be a global brand," he said, "in the same genre as Coke and Disney."

To make that happen, Schultz stepped back from day-to-day operations of the company, handing the title of chief executive officer (CEO) to longtime president Orin Smith. He, meanwhile, became known as the chief global strategist. Schultz's job from there on out would be to establish Starbucks in Europe and beyond.

"Almost anywhere in the world, even in Beijing, you can see one Starbucks outlet from another. They've raised store density to a level I've never seen before."

FINANCIAL ANALYST JOHN GLASS

Starbucks opened its first store in Dubai in 2000; others, like this one in a shopping mall, soon followed.

A BROOKLYN BOY

Howard Schultz grew up in a poor neighborhood in Brooklyn, New York. His father worked a string of jobs that earned just enough to keep his wife and two kids fed and clothed. Neither of his parents was a coffee connoisseur; his mother, he said, would percolate a pot for company but mixed up a cup of instant Maxwell House for herself. Schultz himself didn't think much about it either until, in his 20s, he found himself in Seattle, checking out Starbucks, a small company that had ordered an inordinate number of drip coffeemakers from the company he worked for at the time. One of the employees made him a fresh cup of coffee and handed it to him in a steaming porcelain mug. His eyes bulged at the first sip. Although the Starbucks employees laughed at his reaction to the bitter brew, he kept sipping. "By the third sip, I was hooked," he said.

CHAPTER FIVE

Beyond Coffee

I n March 2001, Starbucks began its methodical march through Europe. It started by building a beautiful, three-story store in Zurich, Switzerland— which claims to be the birthplace of European coffee— that opened to rave reviews on March 7.

"The opening of the first Starbucks store in Zurich is a celebration of Starbucks' successful and passionate history in enriching the coffee and cafe culture worldwide," said Beat Curti, the founder of Bon appétit Group, which partnered with Starbucks on Swiss operations. "I firmly believe that Starbucks will quickly become part of the daily lives of the Swiss people."

Before the year was out, six more Starbucks had been opened in Switzerland; by December, it also had a location in Vienna, Austria. Stores were opened in Germany, Spain, and Greece in 2002, followed by Turkey and France in 2004. Within two years, the company opened more than 650 stores in six countries—most of them in places where coffee cafes had been part of the culture for decades. Although the company worried about how it would be received, it found that most Europeans eagerly embraced the chain.

Between its growing European locations and its stronghold in Asia—in 2003, it opened its 1,000th Asia-Pacific store in Beijing, China—the total number of

Starbucks opened its first French store in Paris in 2004 in the midst of its aggressive European expansion

Starbucks skyrocketed. From 2000 to 2003, the company added almost 4,000 new stores, an average of about five store openings a day. By the end of 2006, the total number of Starbucks locations would jump to more than 12,000. In Starbucks' home state of Washington alone, there would be almost 600 stores—one location for every 11,000 people, compared with one for every 37,000 in the rest of the country.

Such rapid growth prompted some observers to compare Starbucks to McDonald's, the fast-food giant with more than 30,000 restaurants around the world. In 2002, the chain's profits plunged after years of aggressive expansion. Starbucks investors began to worry that, like McDonald's, the coffee company was coming dangerously close to its **saturation** point and that its sales would start to slide. "Starbucks has been very adept at managing its growth, but for a long time McDonald's was as well," said John Owens, an analyst for the investment research firm Morningstar.

Such concerns were not unfounded: Although Starbucks reported a net revenue of $2 billion for the fourth **quarter** of 2006—up 21 percent over the previous year—**same-store sales** fell to their lowest point in years. But Starbucks, company officials said, wouldn't face the same problems McDonald's had. The two businesses were too different to compare, they claimed. "We're in a position to have far more outlets than they could ever have," said Ken Redding, Starbucks vice president of business development. "How many people are going to walk into McDonald's every day and buy a Big Mac and fries? Not many. But a lot more people walk into Starbucks four or five times a week and get a cup of coffee."

Then, just weeks after the company announced its plans to open an additional 2,400 stores in 2007, including its first 10 in Russia, Starbucks founder Howard Schultz sent a memo titled "The **Commoditization** of the Starbucks Experience" to the company's leadership team. In it, he questioned decisions he and others had made for the sake of growth, fearing that they had changed

Starbucks' global reach extended even into the Forbidden City, the great imperial palace in Beijing, China

the Starbucks coffee experience from something special to a common, unremarkable event. "In order to achieve the growth, development, and scale necessary to go from less than 1,000 stores to 13,000 stores and beyond, we have had to make a series of decisions that, in retrospect, have [led] to the watering down of the Starbucks experience, and, what some might call the commoditization of our brand," Schultz wrote.

Automatic espresso machines, bagged coffee beans, and cookie-cutter store design had diluted much of the romance that drinking a cup of fresh coffee in a Starbucks store once had. The stores, Schultz said, felt almost sterile. It was time to get back to Starbucks' roots, to reignite the passion that had fueled the business from its beginning.

Schultz's memo led to a drop in Starbucks' stock prices and to speculation that the company might slow its anticipated growth. But Schultz was adamant that his memo in no way called for a slowdown and confirmed the company's long-term goal to open as many as 40,000 outlets worldwide. As new stores opened in Romania and Russia in 2007, Starbucks also rolled out plans to launch a record label featuring former Beatles star Paul McCartney and other top musicians. It also announced that it would be building a new roasting plant in South Carolina by 2009, the fifth such plant in operation around the world.

Starbucks has been unwavering in its commitment to serve the best possible coffee drinks made from freshly roasted coffee beans, even as the original roster of six stores in Seattle has turned into more than 10,000 outlets across the country and the world. Starbucks has stayed focused on creating an enjoyable coffee experience for its customers, which has made the company that started as a small regional retailer two decades ago one of the most recognizable brands in the world—just as Howard Schultz promised it would.

> *"We continue to believe that Starbucks is a great company and that it is unlikely there will be another company in the coffee category with the brand loyalty and financial strength that the company has."*
>
> FINANCIAL ANALYST HOWARD PENNEY

The solo album worthy of his musical legacy.

Limited Edition
PAUL MCCARTNEY
Starbucks Card

Hear Music, Starbucks' record label, gained instant credibility by signing musician Paul McCartney

BIG-TIME BENEFITS

Starbucks has placed a premium on the contributions of part-time employees to the company by offering them a benefits package similar to that which full-time employees receive. Besides receiving a complimentary pound (.45 kg) of coffee each week and a free drink each shift, employees who work at least 20 hours a week are also eligible for a health care plan with dental and vision benefits. They have the option to contribute to a 401(k) retirement savings plan and are eligible for stock options. CEO Howard Schultz implemented the plan in 1988; in 1994, he was invited to the White House to tell then-president Bill Clinton how he made such an innovative idea work. By 2005, he was back in Washington, D.C., urging lawmakers to help businesses deal with ever-increasing health care costs, saying that his company spent more on insurance for its employees than it did on coffee beans that year.

GLOSSARY

acquiring purchasing a business or other entity, often to add to the assets of another business

baristas people who make espresso coffee as a profession

brand the name of a product or manufacturer; a brand distinguishes a product from similar products made by other manufacturers

bottom line gross (total) sales minus taxes, interest, depreciation, and other expenses; it is also referred to as net earnings or net income

commoditization the process by which a product reaches a point in its development where one brand can't be differentiated from other brands

espresso a strong coffee brewed by forcing steam under pressure through darkly roasted, powdered coffee beans

initial public offering the first sale of stock by a company to the public; it is generally done to raise funds for the company, which is then owned by investors rather than an individual or group of individuals

investors people or companies that put money into a company and then share in any profits the company enjoys or losses it suffers

joint venture a contractual agreement joining together two or more parties to complete a business undertaking; all parties share in whatever profits or losses result

marketing advertising and promoting a product in order to increase sales

mom-and-pop small, independent businesses operated by individual owners; many times, those owners are a husband-and-wife team who handle most of the business responsibilities themselves

NASDAQ an acronym for the National Association of Securities Dealers Automated Quotation system; it is a computerized system used to trade shares in public companies

prototype the first working model of a new product; a prototype is usually improved before being produced in great numbers for sale

quarter one of four three-month intervals that together comprise the financial year; public companies must report certain data on a quarterly basis

same-store sales sales in individual stores in a retail chain that have been open for more than one year, measured without regard to stores that have recently opened

saturation a stage in the life cycle of a product or industry in which everyone who might want the product already has it

seed money money used or needed to set up a new business or enterprise

ticker symbol a three- or four-letter abbreviation used to identify a stock in newspapers, television broadcasts, and on the floor of the stock exchange

SELECTED BIBLIOGRAPHY

Allison, Melissa. "Super Sizing Starbucks." *The Seattle Times* (Sept. 10, 2006): E. 1.

Michelli, Joseph. *The Starbucks Experience: 5 Principles for Turning Ordinary into Extraordinary.* New York: McGraw-Hill, 2006.

Pendergrast, Mark. "The Starbucks Experience: Going Global." *Tea & Coffee Trade Journal* 176, no. 2 (2002).

Schultz, Howard, and Doris Jones Yang. *Pour Your Heart into It: How Starbucks Built a Company One Cup at a Time.* New York: Hyperion Books, 1997.

Stark, John. "Starbucks: At the Helm of Seattle's Espresso Adulation." *Tea & Coffee Trade Journal* (April 1, 1991).

INDEX